SCHIRMER
PERFORMANCE
EDITIONS

HAL LEONARD PIANO LIBRARY

SHOSTAKOVICH

CHILDREN'S NOTEBOOK
Opus 69

Edited by Richard Walters

Fingerings are by the composer, except
those in parentheses are editorial additions.

On the cover:
Autumn (School) (1907)
by Marianne von Werefkin (1860–1938)
(Marianna Vladimirovna Verëvkina)

ISBN 978-1-4950-8338-9

G. SCHIRMER, Inc.

DISTRIBUTED BY

HAL•LEONARD®
7777 W. BLUEMOUND RD. P.O. BOX 13819 MILWAUKEE, WI 53213

Copyright © 2017 by G. Schirmer, Inc. (ASCAP) New York, NY
International Copyright Secured. All Rights Reserved.

Warning: Unauthorized reproduction of this publication is
prohibited by Federal law and subject to criminal prosecution.

www.musicsalesclassical.com
www.halleonard.com

CONTENTS

BIOGRAPHY

DMITRI SHOSTAKOVICH (1906–1975, RUSSIAN)

A major 20th-century composer, Shostakovich is famous for his epic symphonies, concertos, operas, string quartets, and other chamber works. Born in St. Petersburg, his entire career took place in Soviet-era Russia. He was an exceptional musician, demonstrating mastery of sight-singing and memorization at an early age. As a pianist, Shostakovich performed concertos by Mozart, Prokofiev, and Tchaikovsky early in his career, but after 1930 he limited himself to performing his own works and some chamber music.

In 1934, his opera *Lady Macbeth of the Mtsensk District* met with great popular success, but was banned by Stalin for the next thirty years as modernist, surrealist, and obscene. The following year, Stalin began a campaign known as the Purges, executing or exiling to prison camps politicians, intellectuals, and artists who did not sufficiently adhere to the Soviet ideals of socialist realism. Many of Shostakovich's friends and relatives were captured or killed. For several decades, Shostakovich teetered between receiving high official honors and living with an almost debilitating fear of arrest for works that might be seen as too subversive. His more conservative and traditional Fifth Symphony, Op. 47, helped him to regain favor, interpreted by critics as a Soviet artist finally falling in line.

Photo by Roger & Renate Rössing

While continuing to compose "public" pieces like his symphonies, which he knew would be heard by the authorities, he experimented in more intimate forms like the string quartet, where he poured out some of his most personal sentiments. Meanwhile, he taught composition and orchestration at the Leningrad Conservatory from 1937–1968, with brief breaks due to war and other political disruptions, and at the Moscow Conservatory in the 1940s. Later in life Shostakovich suffered two heart attacks and a form of polio in his right hand, which left him unable to play the piano. He died of lung cancer in 1975.

Despite the atmosphere of anxiety and repression, Shostakovich composed an astounding number of works with originality, humor, and emotional power. He succeeded in striking a balance between modernism and tradition that continues to make his music accessible to a broad audience. Since his death in 1975, Shostakovich has become one of the most-performed 20th century composers. His works for solo piano include a cycle of *24 Preludes and Fugues*, Op. 87, modeled on Bach's *Well-Tempered Clavier*, another set of *24 Preludes*, Op. 34, and two sonatas.

CHILDREN'S NOTEBOOK FOR PIANO, OP. 69

(COMPOSED 1944–45)

In 1941, the composer was unwillingly evacuated from his home in Leningrad (St. Petersburg) and moved to Moscow, as were many Russian politicians and prominent celebrities as the Nazi army drew closer to the Russian border. The blockade was lifted in January of 1944 and the family was able to return to visit in October of that year. It was in the months leading up to the hope of returning permanently to Leningrad that Shostakovich composed these short pieces. But returning was not in the future for the family. The Shostakovich family's living situation was likely out of their control when Stalin arranged for them two apartments in the city and a small house in the suburbs of Moscow. They remained in these for over 15 years.

Unlike his contemporary Dmitri Kabalevsky, Shostakovich wrote only a few pieces for piano students. *Children's Notebook for Piano* was written for his eight-year-old daughter, Galina, for her studies on the instrument. The composer promised his daughter he would write a new piece for her each time she mastered one. Galina recalled later that it took her about a month or more to learn each piece. She studied piano and composition with her father for a short time, but did not pursue music into maturity. In 1945 at the Composers' Union in Moscow, Galina gave the first performance of the first six movements. She commented that a memory slip abruptly ended her performance and her father had to finish the work's premiere. Other accounts tell that she performed the "March" and her father performed the remainder of the movements. Later that year, Shostakovich was asked to be the editor for a radio program aimed at teaching children about music. On the first broadcast, he performed this set and lectured on the importance of music. The original set was published as six pieces. The seventh piece, "Birthday," written for Galina's ninth birthday, was added in a later edition after the composer's death (1983). Dmitri gave the first performance of the entire set May 26, 1947 in a live radio broadcast from Prague. For this performance from which a recording is extant, Shostakovich reverses the order of "The Bear" and "Sad Tale." This recording has also been used as a reference for tempo markings for the Collected Works edition, since Shostakovich did not include tempo markings in his original score.

"The Mechanical Doll" uses themes from *Scherzo in F-sharp minor*, Op. 1 for orchestra. "Birthday" foreshadows the opening fanfare from *Festive Overture* in A Major, Op. 96 composed two years later. "The Bear" and "Merry Tale" contain some passages where the hands play parallel figures an octave apart, a hallmark of Shostakovich's piano writing. All seven pieces display Shostakovich's skill in modulating to remote keys and returning to the tonic, even within the compressed length of children's literature. Like Kabalevsky, Shostakovich was not afraid to introduce young pianists to the musical language of the day and to practice fine compositional craft, no matter the project.

Other pieces from this time period include the Second String Quartet, Op. 68, and the Ninth Symphony, Op. 70.

References

Fay, Laurel E. (2005). *Shostakovich: A Life*. Oxford University Press.

Moshevich, Sofia (28 May 2015). *Shostakovich's Music for Piano Solo: Interpretation and Performance*. Indiana University Press.

PRACTICE AND PERFORMANCE TIPS

March

Practice and Performance Tips

- Pay attention to dynamic contrast from the *diminuendo* in measures 7–8 to the sudden f at measure 9, and then again from measures 11–12 to the f at 13.
- A march requires a particularly steady beat. Begin with a slow practice tempo.
- Use no pedal at all.

Waltz

Practice and Performance Tips

- The melody is in the right hand throughout; the left hand is accompaniment.
- Play the right-hand melody with slightly more volume than the left hand.
- In measure 20 the melody lands on a B-flat – the first black note in the piece and the entrance to a new key area. Try a color change here to make it more special.
- The piece could be very well played with no pedal throughout, or careful touches of pedal could be added.

The Bear

Practice and Performance Tips

- This light-hearted, comical piece seems to capture a bear at mischievous play, or maybe a circus bear.
- Practice hands separately first.
- The f sections should have a buoyant touch, even though playing loudly.
- Make the most of the sudden changes from f to p and back to f.
- Any sustaining pedal would spoil the crisp rhythm of this piece. Use no pedal at all.

Merry Tale

Practice and Performance Tips

- Practice hands separately, first at a slow tempo.
- Learn the composer's articulations (staccato, slurs) from the beginning, not added later.
- In measures 1–3 in the right hand, make a distinction between the staccato eighth notes and the non-accented quarter notes.
- After hands-alone practice, move to slow practice with hands together, retaining the articulation you have already learned.
- In this piece there are several 4-bar phrases that sound similar but have subtle differences. Compare measures 1–4, 9–12, and 33–36, as well as measures 17–20 and 25–28.
- This piece needs a crisp, light touch, even in f sections.
- Any sustaining pedal would completely spoil the texture of the music. Use no pedal.

Sad Tale

Practice and Performance Tips

- The composer's marking of *legato sempre* indicates that the entire piece should be played smoothly.
- Begin practice slowly, hands separately.
- Strive for an evenness in tone in smoothly moving from note to note, without the help of the pedal.
- Measure 13 is a classic Shostakovich key change. Make it special!
- Feel the richness of the low range starting at measure 50. Imagine this as a passage scored for cellos and basses in one of Shostakovich's symphonies.

The Mechanical Doll

This piece is occasionally known by other translated titles, such as "The Clockwork Doll."

Practice and Performance Tips

- Begin practice hands separately, and at a slow tempo.
- Divide the piece into sections for your practice. For instance: section 1 measures 1–16; section 2 measures 17–29; section 3: measures 30–45.
- Notice the imitation in measures 5-6, then again in measures 34–35, as the left hand follows the right hand with a similar phrase.
- Learn the articulation (slurs, staccato, accents) as you learn the notes and rhythms.
- When the left hand has the main melody in measures 30–33, it should sound just as strong and independent as when the right hand had the melody earlier.
- Move to practicing hands together, at a slow tempo, retaining the articulations you have learned when practicing hands alone.
- Keep a strict tempo, no matter what the speed.
- Be careful to observe the specific dynamics that are composed.
- Use no pedal at all. This music needs a crisp, playful touch throughout. Pedal would spoil the texture.

Birthday

Practice and Performance Tips

- The eighth-note triplet staccato chords in measures 1, 3, 5, and later in measures 48–50, should be played with a crisp, buoyant bounce. Keep your wrists relaxed and avoid tension.
- After the introduction "fanfare," the music settles into a rather languid waltz in measure 7.
- Practice hands separately, paying careful attention to the composer's slurs and staccato markings.
- Divide the piece into sections for practice. Section 1: measures 1-6; Section 2: measures 7–16; Section 3: measures 17–24; Section 4: measures 24–40; Section 4: measures 41–48; Section 5: measures 48–54.
- Do not forget the general festive spirit of celebration.

— Richard Walters, *editor*
Brendan Fox, Joshua Parman, *assistant editors*

THE PIANO WORKS OF DMITRI SHOSTAKOVICH

Eight Preludes, Op. 2 (1919–1920)

Minuet, Prelude and Intermezzo (1919–1920)

"Murzilka" (1920)

Five Preludes (1920–1921)

Three Fantastic Dances, Op. 5 (1922)

Suite in F-sharp minor for two pianos, Op. 6 (1922)

Sonata No. 1, Op. 12 (1926)

Aphorisms, ten pieces, Op. 13 (1927)

Polka from *The Golden Age*, Op. 22

Twenty-Four Preludes, Op. 34 (1932–1933)

Nocturne – *The Limpid Stream*, Op. 39

Sonata No. 2 in B minor, Op. 61 (1943)

Children's Notebook, six pieces, Op. 69 (1944–1945)

Merry March for two pianos (1949)

Twenty-Four Preludes and Fugues, Op. 87 (1950–1951)

Dances of the Dolls (1952)

Concertino for two pianos in A minor, Op. 94 (1953)

Short piece, Op. 97a

Spanish dance, from *The Gadfly*, Op. 97b

Eleven Variations on a Theme by Glinka, Op. 104a (1957)

CHILDREN'S NOTEBOOK

Opus 69

CHILDREN'S NOTEBOOK
ДЕТСКАЯ ТЕТРАДЬ
March
Марш

Dmitri Shostakovich
Дмитрий Шостакович
Op. 69

Fingerings are by the composer.

Copyright © 1945 by G. Schirmer, Inc. (ASCAP) New York, NY
International Copyright Secured.   All Rights Reserved.

Waltz
Вальс

Fingerings are by the composer.

Copyright © 1945 by G. Schirmer, Inc. (ASCAP) New York, NY
International Copyright Secured.   All Rights Reserved.

4

The Bear
Медведь

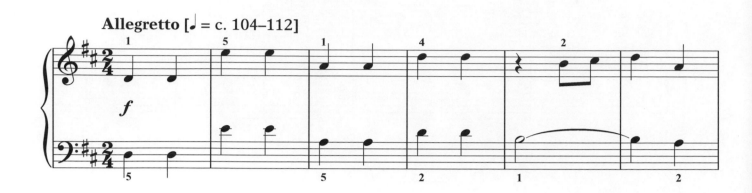

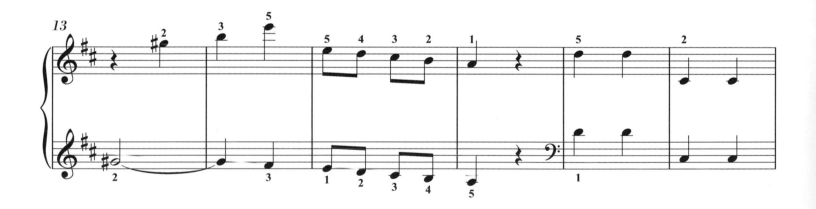

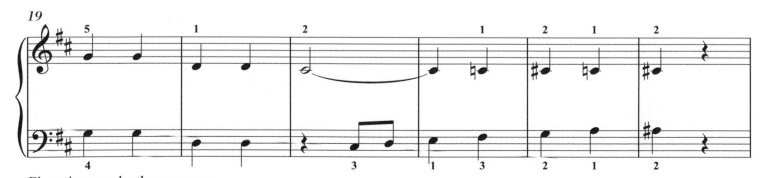

Fingerings are by the composer.

Copyright © 1945 by G. Schirmer, Inc. (ASCAP) New York, NY
International Copyright Secured.   All Rights Reserved.

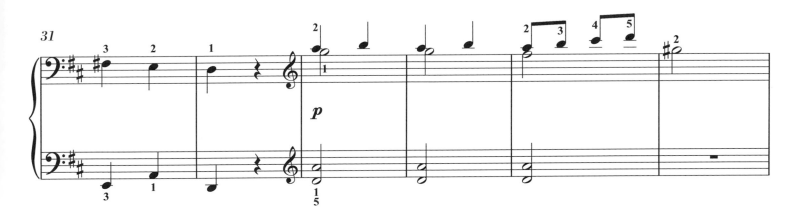

6

Merry Tale
Веселая сказка

Fingerings are by the composer.

Copyright © 1945 by G. Schirmer, Inc. (ASCAP) New York, NY
International Copyright Secured. All Rights Reserved.

Sad Tale
Грстная сказка

Fingerings are by the composer.

Copyright © 1945 by G. Schirmer, Inc. (ASCAP) New York, NY
International Copyright Secured.   All Rights Reserved.

The Mechanical Doll
Заводная кукла

Fingerings are editorial suggestions.

Copyright © 1945 by G. Schirmer, Inc. (ASCAP) New York, NY
International Copyright Secured.   All Rights Reserved.

Birthday
День рождения

Fingerings are editorial suggestions.

Copyright © 1945 by G. Schirmer, Inc. (ASCAP) New York, NY
International Copyright Secured. All Rights Reserved.